2026

Year of the Fire Horse

A Feng Shui Guide to Creating Your Best Year Yet

ANA BARRETO

Copyright © 2025 Ana Barreto
1st Edition, February 2025
ISBN-13: 979-8-9918508-3-4

Blue Hudson Group, Albany, NY

Visit http://www.ana-barreto.com for meditations, classes, and inspirational content.

WORKS BY ANA BARRETO

Sleep Well With Feng Shui: *Transform Your Nights, Transform Your Life*

The Umbrella Effect: *A Journey of Self-Mastery for Women Leaders*

Embrace Your Success: *8 Tools to Improve the Quality of Your Life*

Soul Compass: *A Journal for Intentional Living Through Self-Discovery*

Breaking Free from Self-Sabotage: *A Woman's Guide to Embracing Her Power*

The Nine Powers of Women: *Awakening the Divine Feminine Within*

There is a Higher Power Within: *28 Meditation Prompts to Find Peace & Happiness Within*

Self-Trust: *A Healing Practice for Women Who Do Too Much*

Women, Rice and Beans: *Nine Wisdoms I Learned from My Mother When I Really Paid Attention*

PROGRAMS BY ANA BARRETO

Return to Self: *Unlock Your Full Potential*

The Soul Compass Lab: *15 Weeks to Clarity and Intentional Living*

Visit *www.ana-barreto.com/working-together*

Visit *www.bmwisdom.org* **for online courses and more**

HOW TO CONNECT ONLINE:

Visit http://www.ana-barreto.com for meditations, classes, and inspirational content, and send emails to ana@ana-barreto.com.

Follow me on Facebook, Instagram, and Pinterest: @anabarretoAuthor

Follow me on LinkedIn: @AnaChavesBarreto

Free Gift: The Fire Horse Meditation

To help you thrive in 2026, enjoy my Fire Horse Meditation, a short, powerful practice designed to ground your energy, clear emotional clutter, and align you with the fast, transformative momentum of the Fire Horse year. Use it anytime you need to reset, refocus, and reconnect with your inner strength.

Download it at https://shorturl.at/aeaAy

"I dedicate this book to humanity,

that we may grow in wisdom, flourish in prosperity,

and thrive in health."

Table of Contents

INTRODUCTION

A Brief Story Before the New Year Begins

"I welcome the Fire Horse with clarity, courage, and an open heart. I am ready for the year that will reveal my true strength."

On February 17, 2026, something extraordinary happens.

We step into the Year of the Fire Horse, a year that comes around only once every 60 years.

The Fire Horse carries energy so intense and transformative that it has shaped history, influenced birth rates, and changed the course of countless lives.

Fiery. Independent. Fast-moving. Intensely ambitious.

The Fire Horse favors people who are aligned, grounded, and emotionally steady. It magnifies confidence, courage, boldness, and momentum...

But here's what you must understand: it also magnifies chaos, drama, and disorder when life is out of balance.

WHAT HAPPENED IN 1966

The last Fire Horse year was 1966. In that year, something unprecedented happened across Asia.

Birth rates dropped dramatically.

Not because of poverty or hardship, but because families feared the intensity of Fire Horse children.

Thousands of women chose not to carry their pregnancies. Not because these babies were "bad," but because the energy of the Fire Horse makes children powerful, independent, and uncontainable, sometimes overshadowing the entire family system.

Parents worried: *Will this child be too wild? Too rebellious? Too much for us to handle?*

But here is the truth that changes everything:

Fire Horse energy is only "dangerous" when you are unprepared.

When you are aligned (spiritually, emotionally, physically, and energetically), it becomes the most empowering year of your life.

WHAT THIS GUIDE WILL DO FOR YOU

This isn't a book about superstition or fear.

This is a practical, actionable guide to help you prepare for one of the most dynamic years you will ever experience.

Starting now until February 16, 2026, you have sacred preparation time. After February 17, 2026, until February 5, 2027, you will live the year of the Fire Horse. What you do in these months will determine whether the Fire Horse throws you or carries you forward with unstoppable momentum.

In the pages ahead, you will:

- Understand the Fire Horse energy and how it will influence 2026.
- Assess the nine key areas of your life using the ancient Bagua map.

- Take 28 specific actions to clear, heal, and align your energy for the year of the Fire Horse.
- Discover how your Chinese zodiac sign interacts with the Fire Horse.
- Adjust your space based on your personal north star that influences your daily life.
- Learn powerful rituals for welcoming this energy with grace and intention.
- Create an action plan to enter 2026 prepared, grounded, and confident, and stay that way.

This guide will help you do exactly that.

CHAPTER ONE

Understanding the Fire Horse Energy

"I rise with the flames of change. What is ready to grow in me will grow. What is ready to fall away will fall."

THE CHINESE ZODIAC AND THE 60-YEAR CYCLE

The Chinese zodiac operates on a 12-year cycle, with each year governed by one of twelve animals: Rat, Ox, Tiger, Rabbit, Dragon, Snake, Horse, Goat, Monkey, Rooster, Dog, and Pig.

But there's more to the system than just animals.

Each animal year is also influenced by one of the Five Elements: Wood, Fire, Earth, Metal, or Water. These elements rotate through the zodiac, creating a complete cycle that takes 60 years to complete.

This means that a Fire Horse year, where the Horse meets the Fire element, only occurs once every six decades.

The last Fire Horse year was 1966. The next will be 2086.

2026 is your only chance in this lifetime to harness this energy.

WHAT MAKES FIRE HORSE ENERGY DIFFERENT

The Horse, by nature, is:

- Independent and freedom-loving
- Fast-moving and action-oriented
- Passionate and charismatic
- Intuitive and spirited
- Restless and sometimes impulsive

When you add the **Fire element** to this already dynamic energy, everything intensifies:

Fire brings:

- Amplified passion and courage

- Rapid transformation and change
- Heightened visibility and recognition
- Increased emotional intensity
- Acceleration of whatever is already in motion

Think of it this way: The Fire Horse doesn't walk, **it gallops**. It doesn't whisper, **it roars**. It doesn't, **it acts**.

THE AMPLIFICATION EFFECT: WHY PREPARATION MATTERS

Here's the most important thing you need to understand about 2026:

The Fire Horse magnifies everything.

If your health is strong, it will support you through tremendous growth. If you neglect your health, you'll feel the strain intensely.

If your relationships are loving, they'll deepen and flourish. If your relationships are strained, conflicts will surface more quickly.

If your finances are organized, abundance flows more easily. If your finances are chaotic, the stress will multiply.

If your career is aligned with your purpose, doors will open rapidly. If you're stuck in the wrong job, the misery will become unbearable.

The Fire Horse doesn't create your problems; it reveals them.

And this is actually a gift. (really!)

Because when something is magnified, you can no longer ignore it. You must deal with it. And when you deal with it *before* the year begins, you position yourself to receive all the blessings this powerful energy has to offer.

THE TWO PATHS THROUGH A FIRE HORSE YEAR

There are two ways people experience a Fire Horse year:

Path 1: The Unprepared

- Feel overwhelmed by the speed of change
- Experience conflict, drama, and chaos
- Make impulsive decisions that they later regret
- Feel exhausted and burned out
- Struggle to keep up with life's demands

Path 2: The Prepared

- Experience breakthrough momentum
- Attract opportunities effortlessly
- Feel confident and clear in their choices
- Achieve goals they've been working toward for years
- Ride the energy with grace, strength, and joy

The difference between these two paths is not luck. **It's preparation.**

WHY FEBRUARY 17, 2026, IS THE TURNING POINT

In the Chinese calendar, the new year doesn't begin on January 1. It begins with the Lunar New Year, which falls on a different date each year, always between January 21 and February 20.

In 2026, the Lunar New Year falls on **February 17**.

This is the moment when the Fire Horse officially takes the reins.

Everything you do between now and that date is preparation. It's your window to clear the old, strengthen the weak, and align the misaligned.

After February 17, the energy shifts. The year is in motion. The Horse is running.

You want to be ready before it starts.

THE BUDDHIST LEGEND: HOW THE ZODIAC WAS BORN

Before we dive into the practical work ahead, let me share the ancient story of how the Chinese zodiac came to be. This legend reminds us that the zodiac isn't just a system; it's a spiritual map, rooted in wisdom, compassion, and the natural order of life.

WHEN THE ANIMALS WENT TO SAY GOODBYE TO BUDDHA

Long ago, as the Buddha prepared to leave the earthly realm and enter Nirvana, he sent a gentle message to all living creatures:

"Come to me before my final departure, so I may bless you and honor your spirit."

The animals heard the call carried across forests, fields, and rivers. Some hurried with devotion; others moved at their natural pace; some didn't come at all. But the twelve who arrived became the foundation of the zodiac we still follow today.

THE FIRST TO ARRIVE: THE RAT AND THE OX

Before dawn, the tiny Rat began the journey, but the road was long, and the river was too wide. Knowing he had no chance of reaching Buddha on time, he found the gentle Ox grazing nearby and quietly asked for help.

The Ox, kind as always, offered to carry him across.

When they arrived, the Rat jumped from the Ox's back and bowed before Buddha first.

The Rat became the first sign, and the Ox became the second.

THE TIGER AND THE RABBIT

The Tiger, swift and courageous, fought through the rushing river to arrive third.

The Rabbit, clever and light-footed, hopped across stones and floating logs to arrive in fourth place.

THE DRAGON

The Dragon could have flown straight to Buddha, but along the way, he stopped to help villagers suffering from drought. He brought them rain, then resumed his journey, arriving in 5th place.

THE SNAKE AND THE HORSE

The Horse approached at full speed, but just before entering, he was startled by a quiet presence.

The Snake, who had been coiled peacefully nearby, slipped in ahead, earning 6th place.

The Horse followed as the seventh sign.

THE GOAT, MONKEY, AND ROOSTER

These three arrived together. They had helped one another cross a river by building a makeshift raft:

- The Rooster found the raft
- The Monkey cleared weeds and branches
- The Goat guided them with steady balance

Buddha honored their teamwork, placing them in eighth, ninth, and tenth place.

THE DOG

The Dog should have arrived sooner—he was an excellent swimmer—but he paused to play in the cool water, arriving joyfully as the eleventh sign.

THE PIG

Last came the Pig, who had stopped for a meal and then taken a short nap. He arrived with an honest heart and received the twelfth and final place.

BUDDHA'S BLESSING

When the twelve animals gathered around him, Buddha smiled with compassion.

He said:

"Because you came to honor me, I will honor you. Each of you will rule over one year in a repeating cycle. Your nature will live in the people born under your sign, and your qualities will guide their destiny."

And so, the cycle of twelve years began, each carrying the spirit, personality, strengths, and lessons of one animal.

This is the zodiac we follow today.

WHAT COMES NEXT

Now that you understand the Fire Horse energy and the sacred origins of the zodiac, it's time to look at your own life.

In Chapter 2, you'll learn about the Bagua, the ancient Feng Shui map that divides your life into nine essential areas. This map will become your blueprint for preparation, showing you exactly where to focus your energy in the months ahead.

Then, in Chapter 3, we'll move through each of the nine life areas one by one, with specific assessment questions and practical actions you can take right now to align yourself with the Fire Horse's powerful momentum. The work begins here.

In Chapters 4, 5, 6, and 7, you will again find additional wisdom to navigate the year of the Fire Horse with ease and flow.

The transformation begins with you.

Ready to map your life and start preparing? Turn to Chapter 2.

CHAPTER TWO

The Bagua Map: Your Life Blueprint

"My home mirrors my inner world. As I bring harmony to my space, I bring harmony to my life."

Before we dive into the practical work ahead, you need to understand the tool that will guide you through this preparation: the Bagua.

The Bagua is the heart of feng shui practice, a tool as mystical as it is practical. This powerful energy map, rooted in ancient Taoist wisdom, reveals how the flow of chi in our spaces influences specific areas of our lives. Chi is the life force that flows through all things.

You may have seen it in stores, online, or in someone's house. The Bagua divides any space into nine sections, each connected to one of the fundamental aspects of life. See the picture below.

The Nine Life Areas of the Bagua based on the Black Sector School of Feng Shui

Think of the Bagua as an octagonal map with eight "gua," or life areas, surrounding a central space represented by the Yin and Yang.

Each area corresponds to a direction and is influenced by one of the Five Elements: Wood, Fire, Earth, Metal, or Water.

In the center lies **Health**, the foundation of all other areas. When this central realm is balanced, it enhances all other aspects of life, just as a strong, healthy body enables us to thrive in every activity.

Here are the nine areas:

1. Health & Well-Being

Your foundation. Without health, nothing else stands strong.

2. Career & Life Path

Your purpose and how you show up in the world.

3. Knowledge & Spirituality

Inner wisdom, education, and personal growth.

4. Family & Ancestry

Your roots, heritage, and family relationships.

5. Wealth & Abundance

Money, prosperity, and financial flow.

6. Recognition & Fame

Visibility, confidence, reputation, and how others see you.

7. Relationships & Love

Romantic partnership, marriage, and intimate connections.

8. Creativity & Children

Creative expression, joy, and children (or projects that are your "babies").

9. Helpful People & Travel

Support, mentors, divine guidance, and movement in your life.

HOW TO USE THE BAGUA

The beauty of the Bagua is that you can apply it to any space, your entire home, a single room, or even your desk.

Here's how:

The bottom area of the Bagua always aligns with the wall of the entrance door.

Whether you're looking at your house, your bedroom, or your office, the entrance is always at the bottom of the Bagua map.

Place the Bagua at the entrance, and the door will be in the Knowledge area, career, or Helpful People, unless your home or room is in a U-shape. That means that a space of the Bagua is missing. But that's another book.

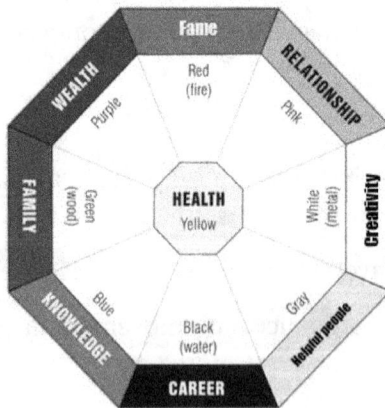

It's easier to use the squares below to visualize the bagua in the room.

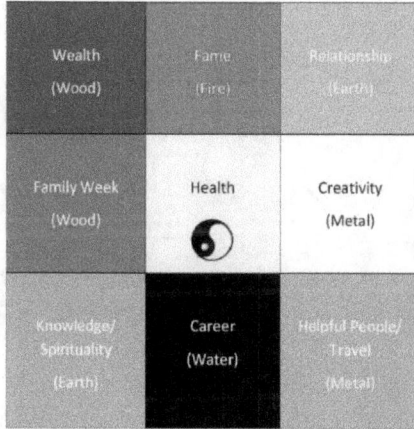

Wealth (Wood)	Fame (Fire)	Relationship (Earth)
Family Week (Wood)	Health	Creativity (Metal)
Knowledge/ Spirituality (Earth)	Career (Water)	Helpful People/ Travel (Metal)

For Your Home: Stand at your front door, looking into your home. The wall with the front door becomes the bottom of the Bagua. The Career area is directly in front of you, Knowledge is to your left, and Helpful People is to your right.

HOW TO LOCATE THE 9 AREAS OF YOUR SPACE

Fame
Finance
Relationship
Family
Health
Creativity
Spirituality
Travel
Career
Entrance Wall

Entrance

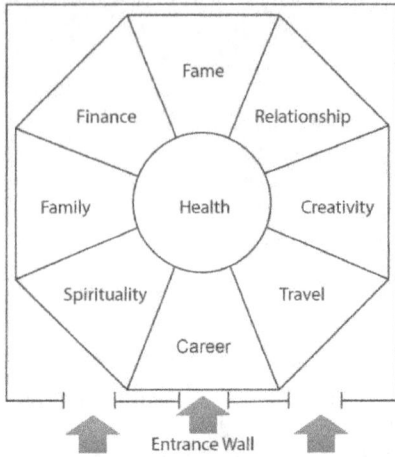

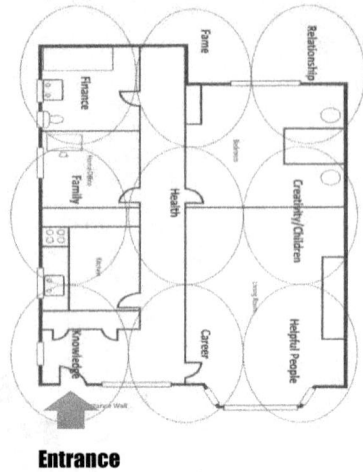

For Your Bedroom: Stand at the bedroom door, looking into the room. That wall becomes the bottom of the Bagua.

For Your Desk: The side where you sit and access the desk is the bottom of the Bagua.

PRACTICE: OVERLAYING THE BAGUA

Get a piece of paper and sketch the layout of your home or the room you want to work on. Mark the entrance.

Now, place the Bagua over your floor plan, with the entrance wall at the bottom.

Each area of the Bagua will fall into a specific corner or section of your room.

Look at what's in each area. Is your Wealth corner cluttered? Is your Relationship area empty, or is it filled with clothes on the floor? Is your Career area blocked by broken or heavy furniture?

The energy of each area directly impacts that aspect of your life.

This is why preparation matters.

Because 2026 will amplify whatever energy already exists in these spaces, you want to make sure each area supports—not blocks—your success.

WHY THIS MATTERS IN A FIRE HORSE YEAR

In 2026, the Fire Horse will magnify the energy in each of these nine areas. Because when something is magnified, you can no longer ignore it. You must deal with it.

If your Health area is cluttered and stagnant, health issues will surface more quickly.

If your Relationship corner is clean and intentional, love will deepen and flourish.

If your Wealth area is broken or blocked, financial stress will intensify.

That's why the next chapter is so important. We're going to move through each of the nine life areas one by one, with specific assessment questions and practical actions you can take *right now* to align yourself with the Fire Horse's powerful momentum.

Remember...

The Fire Horse doesn't create your problems; it reveals them.

CHAPTER THREE

Preparing Your Nine Life Areas

"Every corner I clear, every action I take, becomes a blessing for my future. I prepare my life with intention and love."

Now we get to the work.

Each of the nine areas of your life needs attention before February 17, 2026. You don't have to do everything at once. You don't even have to do everything in this guide. Trust what speaks to you and let go of what doesn't.

But here's what I know: you found this guide because you need the gold nuggets.

For each life area, I'm giving you:

- An affirmation to anchor your intention
- Questions to assess where you are right now
- Three actions (practical and feng shui) you can take before the Fire Horse year begins or if the year has already started, for you to intervene immediately.

I use this practical approach because you need to fully participate in your success. Some people want to use feng shui to attract money, but they don't want to look at their debts or how they spend money. In the year of the Fire Horse, you can't get away from participating in your life. All doors will close, and you will have only a short window to take the appropriate action.

Start where you are. Choose what resonates. And remember that small shifts create big changes when you are working with energy. Do not skip answering the questions. They are designed to connect you with common issues the Fire Horse will address in your life.

3.1 HEALTH & WELL-BEING (Center Bagua)

Affirmation:

"I honor my body, mind, and spirit. My health is my foundation, and I am strong."

Health is your foundation. Without health, nothing else stands strong in a Fire Horse year.

The center of the Bagua governs your physical health, emotional balance, and overall well-being. When this area is clear and strong, every other part of your life benefits.

ASSESSMENT QUESTIONS:

Before you take action, get honest with yourself:

1. When was the last time you had a full health checkup? Are there appointments you've been avoiding?
2. How do you feel when you wake up in the morning? Energized or depleted?
3. Is there clutter under your bed, in your closets, or in the center of your home? (This blocks the flow of healing energy.)
4. What health issue have you been ignoring or "bearing" that you know needs attention?
5. On a scale of 1-10, how would you rate your overall health right now? If it's not a seven rate or above, what do you need to do that you are avoiding?

ACTION 1: GET YOUR HEALTH APPOINTMENTS ON THE CALENDAR

Before the new year, schedule every doctor, dental, and wellness appointment you've been avoiding.

A powerful year requires a powerful vessel.

Don't wait for symptoms to get worse. Don't tell yourself you're "too busy." If you want to ride the Fire Horse with strength, your body needs to be ready.

By putting your health in order, you anchor stability into the Fire Horse's fast-moving energy.

ACTION 2: BRING THE COLOR YELLOW INTO YOUR BEDROOM

Yellow represents health, grounding, and clarity.

Add a yellow throw, pillow, sheets, a bed scarf, or a candle to your bedroom, especially in the center area, if possible.

This simple shift stabilizes the center of your life and strengthens your ability to stay balanced when life accelerates.

You don't need to repaint the entire room. A small touch of yellow is enough to shift the energy.

This is non-negotiable.

Clutter under the bed creates stagnant energy around sleep, healing, and emotional balance. It sits right where your body rests for 6-8 hours every night, blocking the flow of chi.

Clear everything: bins, boxes, shoes, storage, and everything.

Let the Chi circulate freely so your body can truly rest, repair, and reset each night.

If you have a bed with built-in storage drawers, empty and clean them, and put back only what you actually use. Keep them half- or three-quarters-full, never stuffed.

3.2 CAREER & LIFE PATH

Affirmation:
"I am aligned with my purpose. My work flows with ease, and opportunities find me."

The Fire Horse rewards clarity and punishes confusion.

If you're unclear about your career path, 2026 will push you to find it. If you're stuck in work you hate, the misery will intensify. If you're aligned with your purpose, doors will open faster than you can imagine.

ASSESSMENT QUESTIONS:

1. Do you feel aligned with your current job or career? Why or why not?

2. What would you be doing if money weren't an issue?

3. Is there resentment, frustration, or boredom in your work right now?

4. When you think about your career on February 17, 2026, how do you want to feel?

5. Is your workspace organized, clean, and inspiring—or chaotic and draining?

ACTION 4: HEAL YOUR CURRENT JOB BEFORE CHANGING ANYTHING

If you hate your job, 2026 will challenge you.

But before you jump ship, you must clear the energetic residue.

Here's what you do:

Write 20 things you appreciate about your current job (with sincerity.)

Even if you're miserable, find them. The commute is short. You have health insurance. Your coworker makes you laugh. The coffee is free. You learned a skill. Anything.

This simple practice resets your vibration in a powerful way. If you truly want to leave your job, repeat this appreciation exercise daily for about 30 days and mean it. Without this energetic reset, you may attract a new job with the same old problems.

You will either begin liking your job... or you will finally attract the job you truly want.

Complaining keeps you stuck. Appreciation opens the door.

ACTION 5: ADJUST YOUR DESK TO FACE YOUR PERSONAL SUCCESS DIRECTION

In feng shui, your Kua number reveals your favorable directions based on your birth date.

(Note: See the Kua chart in Chapter 4.)

Turn your desk so you're facing your "success" direction when you work. This aligns your mind and energy with opportunity and clarity.

If you can't move your desk, place a small mirror on your desk so you can see the door behind you. This creates a sense of safety and control. If you cannot move, try turning your chair or computer slightly in one of your positive directions.

ACTION 6: HANG A METAL WIND CHIME IN THE CAREER AREA

Metal activates the Water element in the Career area of your home.

This helps dissolve stagnation, attract flow, and create momentum for new professional opportunities.

Hang a small metal wind chime in the Career section of your home (the center bottom area when you stand at the front door looking in).

Let it ring occasionally to keep the energy moving.

3.3 KNOWLEDGE & SPIRITUALITY

Affirmation:

"I trust my inner wisdom. I am open to learning, growing, and evolving."

This is where inner wisdom quiets fear and confusion.

The Knowledge area governs education, self-cultivation, and spiritual practice. When this area is strong, you trust yourself. You make decisions from clarity, not panic.

In a Fire Horse year, you need this inner compass more than ever.

ASSESSMENT QUESTIONS:

1. Do you have a daily practice that connects you to your inner wisdom? (Meditation, prayer, journaling, yoga, etc.)
2. Is there something you've been wanting to learn or study but keep postponing?

3. Do you trust your intuition, or do you second-guess yourself constantly?

4. Is the Knowledge area of your home (front left when you enter) cluttered or empty?

5. How often do you make time for stillness and reflection?

ACTION 7: CREATE A SACRED LEARNING CORNER

In the Knowledge area of your home, place books, journals, meditation tools, or spiritual symbols, but not in your bedroom.

This tells the Fire Horse you are committed to inner mastery, not just outer achievement.

It doesn't have to be elaborate. A small shelf with meaningful items is enough.

ACTION 8: START A 5-MINUTE DAILY REFLECTION PRACTICE

Sit for five minutes each day and ask yourself:

What do I need to understand about myself today?

Write down what comes. Don't judge it. Just listen.

Consistency builds spiritual clarity. Five minutes is enough to change your life.

Earth stabilizes the mind.

Place a crystal, stone, or pottery piece in the Knowledge area of your home.

These grounding objects will help you stay centered when life speeds up.

3.4 FAMILY & ANCESTRY

Affirmation:

"I honor my roots. I release what no longer serves me. I am at peace with my family."

Roots matter more in a Fire Horse year.

The Family area governs your relationships with your parents, siblings, and ancestors, as well as your sense of belonging. Unresolved family tension will surface in 2026. Peace in your heart will multiply.

ASSESSMENT QUESTIONS:

1. Is there unresolved tension or hurt with any family member?
2. Do you carry guilt, shame, or resentment about your family history?
3. When you think about your family, do you feel warmth or heaviness?

4. Are there family photos in your home? Do they bring you joy or sadness?

5. Is the Family area of your home (middle left side) cluttered, broken, or neglected?

ACTION 10: MAKE EMOTIONAL AMENDS

If you have long-standing tension with family members, now is the time to soften it.

You don't need to be close friends. You don't need to eat Thanksgiving together.

But you do need peace in your heart.

Understanding—not agreement—is the goal.

Creating space in your heart for people you understand are simply different.

You can't control their actions, but you can free your body from the emotional weight they trigger.

You could write a letter (you don't have to send it). Forgive them silently. Let it go.

ACTION 11: PLACE HAPPY FAMILY PHOTOS IN THE FAMILY AREA

Choose images from joyful memories—not forced ones.

If you don't have happy family photos, that's okay. You can place images of trees, forests, or ancestors you admire.

This strengthens your emotional roots and creates harmony inside your home.

ACTION 12: ADD LIVING WOOD ENERGY (PLANTS, BAMBOO, FRESH FLOWERS)

Wood represents growth and healing. It nourishes the Family area and supports emotional renewal.

Place a healthy plant, bamboo, or fresh flowers in the Family section of your home.

Keep it alive. Water it. Care for it.

As it grows, so does your capacity for family healing.

3.5 WEALTH & ABUNDANCE

Affirmation:
"I am worthy of abundance. Money flows to me easily. I am financially empowered."

Money is energy, and in a Fire Horse year, it multiplies whatever is already happening.

If you're in debt, it will feel heavier. If you avoid money, the avoidance will cost you. If you're clear and intentional, abundance flows faster.

ASSESSMENT QUESTIONS:

1. Do you know your current financial situation? (Net worth, debts, income, expenses?)
2. How do you feel when you think about money? Anxious? Guilty? Empowered? Or you don't want to think about it?
3. Is there clutter in the Wealth area of your home (back left corner from the entrance)?
4. Do you spend compulsively? Save compulsively? Avoid looking at your bank account?
5. What is your relationship with money, honestly?

ACTION 13: FACE YOUR FINANCIAL REALITY

If you have debt, face it.
If you overspend, face it.
If you avoid money, face it.
If you fear spending, face it.

Because whatever your financial story is right now, it will be amplified in 2026. Use the Horse Fire meditation to help you face your finances.

ACTION 13B: CALCULATE YOUR NET WORTH

No judgment. Just clarity.

Add up everything you own (assets) and subtract everything you owe (debts).

That's your net worth. Allow it to be what it is without feeling guilt or shame. Change starts here. By the way, the year of the Fire Horse is a great year to begin an abundance plan. It's a good time to make a settlement with creditors, open a savings account, begin investing, and more.

Knowing where you stand puts financial power back in your hands.

ACTION 14: PLACE 9 COINS IN YOUR HOME

This is a traditional feng shui remedy for activating wealth.

Collect nine coins (any currency).

- Place three coins outside your front door (under the mat or near the entrance)
- Place three coins inside your front door (in a bowl or under a rug)
- Place three coins in the Wealth corner of your home

Also, collect all loose change in your home and place it in a bowl in the Wealth corner.

PS: You don't activate wealth until you face your full financial situation.

ACTION 15: PLACE A WATER FOUNTAIN IN THE WEALTH AREA

Moving water activates abundance.

If you can, place a small water fountain in the Wealth area of your home. Please keep it clean and running.

If a fountain isn't possible, place a bowl of clean water with fresh flowers.

Also: Clean your wallet. Remove old receipts. Only carry what you love and value inside. If you can, keep a $100 bill in it and don't spend it.

3.6 RECOGNITION & FAME

Affirmation:

"I am visible. I am confident. I am worthy of recognition and success."

Visibility, confidence, and self-respect.

The Fire Horse year will shine a spotlight on you—whether you're ready or not. If you don't see your own value, 2026 will force you to find it.

ASSESSMENT QUESTIONS:

1. Do you feel comfortable being visible and recognized for your work?
2. What accomplishments are you proud of that you've never shared?
3. Do you downplay your success or deflect compliments?
4. Is the Recognition area of your home (back center) vibrant or dim?
5. How do you want to be known in 2026?

ACTION 16: MAKE A LIST OF 20 QUALITIES YOU APPRECIATE ABOUT YOURSELF

If you can't see your qualities, why would anyone else?

Write them down. Read them out loud. Let them sink in.

This practice builds the inner flame that matches the Fire Horse's external power.

ACTION 17: INTRODUCE THE COLOR RED

Red activates success, passion, and recognition.

Add a red candle, pillow, or artwork in the Recognition area of your home or office (back center from the entrance). Don't paint the walls red because it's overkill and invokes the energy of desperation.

You don't need a lot. A small touch of red is enough to ignite the energy.

ACTION 18: DISPLAY YOUR DIPLOMAS, AWARDS, OR CERTIFICATES

Let your accomplishments have a place of honor.

Recognition begins with self-recognition.

If you've been hiding your degrees or achievements, bring them out. Frame them. Display them in the Recognition area of your office or on your personal success directions (See your kua number). You earned them. Own them.

3.7 RELATIONSHIPS & LOVE

Affirmation:

"I am worthy of love. I attract healthy, joyful, supportive relationships into my life."

Love energy must be clear before the year begins.

Whatever you are happy or unhappy about in your relationship, it will magnify during the year of the Fire Horse.

ASSESSMENT QUESTIONS:

1. If you're partnered: Are you happy in your relationship? What does it need to shift?
2. If you're single: Do you feel worthy of love, or do you carry past hurt?
3. Is your bedroom set up for partnership, or does it reflect solitude?
4. Are there images of single people, sad art, or past relationships in your bedroom?
5. What does your heart truly want in love?

ACTION 19: CLARIFY THE ENERGY OF YOUR RELATIONSHIP

If you are partnered:

Write a list of all the qualities you appreciate about your partner.

Appreciation aligns you with truth, not fear. It helps you make decisions from a place of emotional wellness—not exhaustion or frustration.

If you are single:

Write a list of the qualities you bring to a relationship.

When you value yourself, you attract someone who can value you too.

ACTION 20: RESET YOUR BEDROOM

Make your bed every day.

Use equal nightstands on both sides (even if you're single—this creates energetic space for partnership).

Remove clutter, laundry piles, and electronics.

Sleep on one side if you're single to make room for a partner.

If you're in a relationship, make sure both sides of the bed are balanced and welcoming.

ACTION 21: CREATE A LOVE ALTAR

In the Relationship area of your bedroom (back right corner from the door), create a small altar.

Include:

- A happy photo of you (or you + your partner)
- Two red candles
- Heart-shaped stones
- Symbols of joyful love

Remove all religious icons, children's photos, or sad/solitary artwork from the bedroom.

The bedroom is for rest and romance, nothing else.

PS: If you have your office in the bedroom and cannot move it, unplug the electronics at the end of the day and cover the area with a screen or curtain.

3.8 CREATIVITY & CHILDREN

Affirmation:
"I am a creative being. Joy flows through me. I welcome playfulness and inspiration into my life."

Your ideas, joy, and creative expansion.

The Creativity area governs children, creative projects, and anything that brings you joy. In a Fire Horse year, inspiration will strike fast—but only if you make space for it.

ASSESSMENT QUESTIONS:

1. Do you make time for creative play, or is your life all work?
2. If you have children, how is your relationship with them?
3. Are there creative projects you've been wanting to start but keep putting off?
4. Is the Creativity area of your home (middle right) cluttered or stagnant?
5. When was the last time you did something just for fun?

ACTION 22: DECLUTTER YOUR SPACE

Clutter blocks creativity.

Clear old projects, donate unused things, and make space for new inspiration.

If you have unfinished creative projects gathering dust, either finish them or let them go.

ACTION 23: ADD METAL TO ACTIVATE CREATIVITY

Metal frames, bowls, or sculptures strengthen this area and support your fresh ideas.

Place a metal object in the Creativity section of your home (middle right from the entrance).

ACTION 24: START A "JOY LIST"

Write ten creative things you want to explore in 2026—not for productivity, but for pleasure.

Painting. Dancing. Writing. Singing. Gardening. Cooking. Photography.

Creativity expands your energy, which the Fire Horse needs to help you achieve your goals.

Pick one thing from your list and schedule it before February 17.

3.9 HELPFUL PEOPLE & TRAVEL

Affirmation:

"I am supported. The right people and opportunities come to me at the right time."

Support, guidance, and forward movement.

The Helpful People area governs mentors, angels, divine support, and travel. When this area is strong, help arrives when you need it. Doors open. Synchronicities multiply.

ASSESSMENT QUESTIONS:

1. Do you feel supported in your life, or do you feel alone?
2. Are you open to receiving help, or do you insist on doing everything yourself?

3. Is there travel you've been wanting to do but keep postponing?
4. Is your entryway cluttered, dark, or uninviting?
5. Who are the people in your life who truly support you?

ACTION 25: DECLUTTER THE ENTRYWAY OR FRONT DOOR

Your entryway is where new opportunities enter your life.

Clear shoes, old mail, and stagnant energy.

Wipe the door. Add a plant or a welcoming object.

Make it beautiful. Make it inviting.

ACTION 26: CREATE A GRATITUDE LIST FOR THE PEOPLE WHO HELP YOU

Write the names of mentors, helpers, or people who uplift you, and write them a thank-you letter.

Appreciation strengthens the support network around you and attracts new allies.

You don't have to send them the letter. Just write it and feel the gratitude.

ACTION 27: ADD TRAVEL OR SPIRITUAL SYMBOLS

Place a globe, a map, or meaningful travel objects in the Helpful People area (on the front right from the entrance of the house or office) to activate journeys, movement, and new opportunities.

If you desire spiritual guidance, add images of saints, angels, or deities on the far-right section of your entrance wall.

These symbols amplify divine support and strengthen the flow of helpful people, mentors, and uplifting connections for the year ahead.

You've just mapped your entire life.

These 27 actions are your roadmap to a powerful Fire Horse year.

Don't try to do everything at once. Start with the three areas that need your attention most.

Trust your intuition. You know where to begin.

CHAPTER FOUR

Finding Your True North

"When I align with my true direction, life aligns with me. I trust the compass of my spirit."

In a Fire Horse year, you need every advantage you can get.

This chapter gives you one of the most powerful tools in Feng Shui: your **personal directions**.

Unlike traditional Feng Shui, which looks at the energy of a space as a whole, personal Feng Shui considers **your** unique energy blueprint—derived from your birth date and expressed through something called your Kua Number (pronounced "kwah").

KUA NUMBERS

Your Kua Number reveals which directions support your health, success, relationships, and personal growth, and which directions drain your energy or create obstacles.

When you align your bed, desk, and daily activities with your favorable directions, you tap into a natural flow of support. You sleep better. You think clearly. You make better decisions. Opportunities find you more easily.

In the Fire Horse year, this alignment becomes even more critical. The energy moves fast. You need to be positioned to receive it.

Think of it as divine help available to you simply by facing the right way.

FINDING YOUR KUA NUMBER: YOUR UNIQUE ENERGY BLUEPRINT

The Kua Number is calculated from your birth year and varies based on gender. Follow these simple steps to find yours:

For Males:

1. Take the last two digits of your birth year.

2. Add these two digits together until you have a single digit.

3. Subtract this number from 10. The result is your Kua Number.

For Females:

1. Take the last two digits of your birth year.

2. Add these two digits together until you have a single digit.

3. Add 5 to this number. The result is your Kua Number.

Example Calculation:

- For a male born in 1966: 6 + 6 = 12, then 1 + 2 = 3. Subtracting from 10 gives 7, so the Kua Number is **7**.

- For a female born in 1966: 6 + 6 = 12, then 1 + 2 = 3. Adding 5 gives 8, so the Kua Number is **8**.

My Kua Number is: _____

Double-check your Kua number.

To find your Kua Number, check your birthdate and gender in the list below.

YEAR	BIRTHDAY RANGE	MAN	WOMAN
1940:	Feb 8, 1940 - Jan 26, 1941	6	9
1941:	Jan 27, 1941 - Feb 14, 1942	5	1
1942:	Feb 15, 1942 - Feb 4, 1943	4	2
1943:	Feb 5, 1943 - Jan 24, 1944	3	3
1944:	Jan 25, 1944 - Feb 12, 1945	2	4
1945:	Feb 13, 1945 – Feb 1, 1946	1	5
1946:	Feb 2, 1946 - Jan 21, 1947	9	6
1947:	Jan 22, 1947 - Feb 9, 1948	8	7
1948:	Feb 10, 1948 - Jan 28, 1949	7	8
1949:	Jan 29, 1949 - Feb 16, 1950	6	9
1950:	Feb 17, 1950 - Feb 5, 1951	5	1
1951:	Feb 6, 1951 - Jan 26, 1952	4	2
1952:	Jan 27, 1952 - Feb 13, 1953	3	3
1953:	Feb 14, 1953 - Feb 2, 1954	2	4
1954:	Feb 3, 1954 - Jan 23, 1955	1	5
1955:	Jan 24, 1955 - Feb 11, 1956	9	6
1956:	Feb 12, 1956 - Jan 30, 1957	8	7
1957:	Jan 31, 1957 - Feb 17, 1958	7	8
1958:	Feb 18, 1958 - Feb 7, 1959	6	9
1959:	Feb 8, 1959 - Jan 27, 1960	5	1
1960:	Jan 28, 1960 - Feb 14, 1961	4	2
1961:	Feb 15, 1961 - Feb 4, 1962	3	3
1962:	Feb 5, 1962 - Jan 24, 1963	2	4

YEAR	BIRTHDAY RANGE	MAN	WOMAN
1963:	Jan 25, 1963 - Feb 12, 1964	1	5
1964:	Feb 13, 1964 - Feb 1, 1965	9	6
1965:	Feb 2, 1965 - Jan 20, 1966	8	7
1966:	Jan 21, 1966 - Feb 8, 1967	7	8
1967:	Feb 9, 1967 - Jan 29, 1968	6	9
1968:	Jan 30, 1968 - Feb 16, 1969	5	1
1969:	Feb 17, 1969 - Feb 5, 1970	4	2
1970:	Feb 6, 1970 - Jan 26, 1971	3	3
1971:	Jan 27, 1971 - Feb 14, 1972	2	4
1972:	Feb 15, 1972 - Feb 2, 1973	1	5
1973:	Feb 3, 1973 - Jan 22, 1974	9	6
1974:	Jan 23, 1974 - Feb 10, 1975	8	7
1975:	Feb 11, 1975 - Jan 30, 1976	7	8
1976:	Jan 31, 1976 - Feb 17, 1977	6	9
1977:	Feb 18, 1977 - Feb 6, 1978	5	1
1978:	Feb 7, 1978 - Jan 27, 1979	4	2
1979:	Jan 28, 1979 - Feb 15, 1980	3	3
1980:	Feb 16, 1980 - Feb 4, 1981	2	4
1981:	Feb 5, 1981 - Jan 24, 1982	1	5
1982:	Jan 25, 1982 - Feb 12, 1983	9	6
1983:	Feb 13, 1983 - Feb 1, 1984	8	7
1984:	Feb 2, 1984 - Feb 19, 1985	7	8
1985:	Feb 20, 1985 - Feb 8, 1986	6	9

YEAR	BIRTHDAY RANGE	MAN	WOMAN
1986:	Feb 9, 1986 - Jan 28, 1987	5	1
1987:	Jan 29, 1987 - Feb 16, 1988	4	2
1988:	Feb 17, 1988 - Feb 5, 1989	3	3
1989:	Feb 6, 1989 - Jan 26, 1990	2	4
1990:	Jan 27, 1990 - Feb 14, 1991	1	5
1991:	Feb 15, 1991 - Feb 3, 1992	9	6
1992:	Feb 4, 1992 - Jan 22, 1993	8	7
1993:	Jan 23, 1993 - Feb 9, 1994	7	8
1994:	Feb 10, 1994 - Jan 30, 1995	6	9
1995:	Jan 31, 1995 - Feb 18, 1996	5	1
1996:	Feb 19, 1996 - Feb 6, 1997	4	2
1997:	Feb 7, 1997 - Jan 27, 1998	3	3
1998:	Jan 28, 1998 - Feb 15, 1999	2	4
1999:	Feb 16, 1999 - Feb 4, 2000	1	5
2000:	Feb 5, 2000 - Jan 23, 2001	9	6
2001:	Jan 24, 2001 - Feb 11, 2002	8	7
2002:	Feb 12, 2002 - Jan 31, 2003	7	8
2003:	Feb 1, 2003 - Jan 21, 2004	6	9
2004:	Jan 22, 2004 - Feb 8, 2005	5	1
2005:	Feb 9, 2005 - Jan 28, 2006	4	2
2006:	Jan 29, 2006 - Feb 17, 2007	3	3
2007:	Feb 18, 2007 - Feb 6, 2008	2	4
2008:	Feb 7, 2008 - Jan 25, 2009	1	5

YEAR	BIRTHDAY RANGE	MAN	WOMAN
2009:	Jan.26, 2009 – Feb. 2010	9	6
2010:	Feb. 14, 2010 – Feb. 2011	8	7
2011:	Feb. 3, 2011 – Jan. 22, 2012	7	8
2012:	Jan. 23, 2012 – Feb.9, 2013	6	9
2013:	Feb.10, 2013- Jan 30, 2014	5	1
2014:	Jan. 31, 2013- Feb 18, 2015	4	2
2015:	Feb. 19, 2015 – Feb. 7, 2016	3	3
2016:	Feb. 8, 2016 - Jan. 27, 2017	2	4
2017:	Jan. 28, 2017 – Feb. 15, 2018	1	5
2018:	Feb. 16, 2018 – Feb. 4, 2019	9	6
2019:	Feb. 5, 2019 - Jan. 24, 2020	8	7
2020:	Jan. 25, 2020 – Feb.11, 2021	7	8
2021:	Feb.11, 2021 – Jan.31, 2022	6	9
2022:	Feb. 1, 2022 - Jan.21, 2023	5	1
2023:	Jan.22, 2023 – Feb.09, 2024	4	2
2024:	Feb.10, 2024 – Jan.28, 2025	3	3
2025:	Jan,29, 2025 – Feb 16, 2026	2	4
2026:	Feb 17, 2026 – Feb 5, 2027	1	5
2027:	Feb 6, 2027 – Jan 25, 2028	9	6
2028:	Jan 26, 2028 – Feb 12, 2029	8	7
2029:	Feb 13, 2029 – Feb 2, 2030	7	8
2030:	Feb 3, 2030 – Jan 22, 2031	6	9
2031:	Jan 23, 2031 – Feb 10, 2032	5	1

YEAR	BIRTHDAY RANGE	MAN	WOMAN
2032:	Feb 11, 2032 – Jan 30, 2033	4	2
2033:	Jan 31, 2033 – Feb 18, 2034	3	3
2034:	Feb 19, 2034 – Feb 7, 2035	2	4
2035:	Feb 8, 2035 – Jan 27, 2036	1	5

UNDERSTANDING YOUR KUA NUMBER

Once you know your Kua Number, you'll discover your personal archetype (your energetic signature) and the directions that support or challenge you.

Read your description below. Notice what resonates. Then identify your four auspicious (favorable) directions and your four inauspicious (unfavorable) directions.

This is your energetic roadmap for the year ahead.

KUA #1 - THE WEALTH CREATOR

Description: Visionary, strategic, and resourceful, the Wealth Creator is skilled in manifesting prosperity and finding opportunities where others may not see them. They excel in environments that allow them to innovate and build, bringing ideas to fruition. Driven by a natural aptitude for success, they inspire others through their achievements.

Auspicious Directions:

- Success Direction: SE

- Health Direction: E

- Relationship Direction: S

- Wisdom Direction: N

Inauspicious Directions:

- Failure Direction: NW

- Torment Direction: SW

- Problem Direction: NE

- Losses Direction: W

KUA #2 - THE TEACHER

Description: Wise, patient, and grounded, the Teacher is dedicated to nurturing growth and understanding in others. With a strong connection to stability and tradition, they provide guidance and support, imparting knowledge through their experiences. Teachers are dependable and compassionate, thriving in roles that involve sharing wisdom.

Auspicious Directions:

- Success Direction: NE

- Health Direction: W

- Relationship Direction: NW

- Wisdom Direction: SW

Inauspicious Directions:

- Failure Direction: S

- Torment Direction: N

- Problem Direction: E

- Lesson Direction: SE

KUA #3 - THE BRINGER OF LIGHT

Description: Optimistic, charismatic, and energizing, the Bringer of Light brings hope, motivation, and inspiration to those around them. They are naturally inclined to lead and uplift, using their energy to spread positivity and encourage growth. With a flair for connection and enthusiasm, they brighten any environment and inspire others.

Auspicious Directions:

- Success Direction: S

- Health Direction: N

- Relationship Direction: SE

- Wisdom Direction: E

Inauspicious Directions:

- Failure Direction: NW

- Torment Direction: SW

- Problem Direction: W

- Losses Direction: NE

KUA #4 - THE MANAGER

Description: Organized, methodical, and resourceful, the Manager has a natural talent for coordinating people, projects, and resources. They thrive in structured environments and are known for their ability to bring order and efficiency to any situation. Managers are focused and goal-oriented, often excelling in leadership roles.

Auspicious Directions:

- Success Direction: N

- Health Direction: S

- Relationship Direction: E

- Wisdom Direction: SE

Inauspicious Directions:

- Failure Direction: SW

- Torment Direction: NW

- Problem Direction: NE

- Losses Direction: W

Kua #5

If you are a man, use Kua 2, The Teacher. If you are a woman, use Kua 8, The Connector.

Kua #6 - The Creator

Description: Innovative, disciplined, and visionary, the Creator is a natural leader with a strong drive to bring ideas to life. They are strategic and grounded, often initiating projects and inspiring others to follow their lead. With a passion for building and creativity, they excel in environments that allow for both structure and imagination.

Auspicious Directions:

- Success Direction: W

- Health Direction: NE

- Relationship Direction: SW

- Wisdom Direction: NW

Inauspicious Directions:

- Failure Direction: SE

- Torment Direction: E

- Problem Direction: S

- Losses Direction: N

KUA #7 - THE ADVISOR

Description: Intuitive, diplomatic, and insightful, the Advisor has a gift for understanding others' needs and providing wise counsel. They bring harmony to situations, often offering balanced perspectives and solutions. Known for their charm and empathy, Advisors excel in roles that require interpersonal connection and guidance.

Auspicious Directions:

- Success Direction: NW

- Health Direction: SW

- Relationship Direction: NE

- Wisdom Direction: W

Inauspicious Directions:

- Failure Direction: E

- Torment Direction: SE

- Problem Direction: N

- Losses Direction: S

KUA #8 - THE CONNECTOR

Description: Reliable, resilient, and compassionate, the Connector naturally brings people together and fosters community. With a grounded presence, they excel in building meaningful relationships and creating networks. They provide stability to those around them, often serving as a bridge between people and ideas.

Auspicious Directions:

- Success Direction: SW

- Health Direction: NW

- Relationship Direction: W

- Wisdom Direction: NE

Inauspicious Directions:

- Failure Direction: E

- Torment Direction: N

- Problem Direction: S

- Losses Direction: SE

KUA #9 - THE HEALER

Description: Compassionate, empathetic, and deeply intuitive, the Healer is naturally attuned to others' needs and has a calming, restorative presence. They inspire warmth and balance, often providing support and guidance to those around them. With a gift for nurturing and creating harmony, Healers excel in roles that foster healing and connection.

Auspicious Directions:

- Success Direction: E

- Health Direction: SE

- Relationship Direction: N

- Wisdom Direction: S

Inauspicious Directions:

- Failure Direction: W

- Torment Direction: NE

- Problem Direction: SW

- Losses Direction: NW

Write It Down

Now that you know your Kua Number and directions, write them here:

My Kua Number is: _____

My Best Directions are: _____ _____ _____ _____

My Worst Directions are: _____ _____ _____ _____

THE FOUR FAVORABLE DIRECTIONS: WHERE ENERGY SUPPORTS YOU

Now that you know your favorable directions, let's understand what each one offers:

1. Success Direction This is your power direction for achievement, career success, and recognition. Face this direction when you're working, making important decisions, or during focused tasks. This direction supports growth and helps you reach your goals.

2. Health Direction Connected to vitality, longevity, and physical well-being, this direction supports restorative sleep and overall health. Position your bed so your head points in this direction for enhanced energy and healing.

3. Relationship Direction This direction nurtures love, friendships, and social harmony. Face this direction during meaningful conversations, or position relationship-oriented spaces (like your bedroom) in this area to enhance connection and balance.

4. Wisdom Direction This direction supports inner clarity, learning, and spiritual insight. Face this direction while sleeping (as an alternative to your Health direction), meditating, or studying. It fosters problem-solving, mental growth, and a deeper connection to purpose.

When you align with these directions, you naturally enhance the flow of positive energy. Life becomes easier. Decisions become clearer. Success comes more naturally.

THE FOUR UNFAVORABLE DIRECTIONS: WHERE ENERGY WORKS AGAINST YOU

Just as there are directions that support you, there are directions that create resistance. Knowing these helps you avoid, mitigate, or "cure" challenging energy in your home.

1. Failure Direction Associated with obstacles, setbacks, and stagnation. Avoid facing this direction when working, sleeping, or making critical decisions. If your bed or desk must face this way, use calming colors or Feng Shui cures (like plants or crystals) to balance the energy.

2. Torment Direction Brings emotional stress, miscommunications, and conflicts. Avoid aligning relationship-oriented spaces, like bedrooms, with this direction, as it may create tension in close connections.

3. Problem Direction Associated with health concerns, stress, or minor misfortunes. Avoid this direction in spaces where you want relaxation or calm. If unavoidable, soften the energy with calming artwork, plants, or earthy tones.

4. Loss Direction Linked to financial loss or drained energy. Avoid placing workspaces or areas where finances are managed in this direction. Offset with grounding elements, such as plants or soothing colors.

These directions don't need to instill fear; they simply help you make informed choices. By focusing on your favorable directions, you'll naturally avoid the unfavorable ones, creating a more supportive flow of energy.

HOW TO USE THIS KNOWLEDGE: A PRACTICAL GUIDE

Now comes the most important part: applying what you've learned.

Grab a compass (you can download a compass app on your phone) and follow these steps:

Step 1: Check Your Bedroom

Go to the center of your bedroom. Hold your compass flat at heart level.

Turn slowly until you're facing the direction of your headboard (the wall your head points toward when you sleep).

Write down the direction: _____

Is this one of your favorable directions? If yes, excellent. If no, consider repositioning your bed so your head points toward your Health Direction or Wisdom Direction.

Step 2: Check Your Workspace

Go to your desk or wherever you work. Stand where you normally sit.

Face the direction you look while working (not the direction of your back, but where your eyes naturally focus).

Write down the direction: _____

Is this one of your favorable directions, ideally, your Success Direction? If not, rearrange your desk or turn your chair so you face a better direction, as long as your back is not towards the door.

Step 3: Check Your Other Spaces

Do the same for:

- Where do you eat (which direction do you face at the dining table?)

- Where do you relax (which direction do you face on your sofa?)

- Where you meditate or do spiritual practice

Write down these directions and adjust as needed.

Step 4: Make the Changes

You don't have to change everything at once. Start with the two most important spaces: your bed and your desk.

Even small shifts, turning your chair 25-45 degrees, moving your bed to face a different wall, can create noticeable changes in your energy, clarity, and well-being.

This is alignment in action.

A NOTE ON FLEXIBILITY

Sometimes, room layouts make it impossible to face your ideal direction. That's okay.

Do the best you can. If you can't face your Success Direction while working, face your Wisdom Direction instead. If you can't position your bed perfectly, get as close as you can.

The goal isn't perfection; it's awareness and intention.

Every small adjustment brings you closer to alignment.

YOU NOW HAVE YOUR ENERGETIC BLUEPRINT

You know your Kua Number. You know your favorable and unfavorable directions. You know where you sleep, work, and spend time.

Now, make the adjustments.

Face your power. Align with your energy. Let the Fire Horse year work **with** you, not against you.

This is how you prepare—not just by clearing clutter or setting intentions, but by positioning yourself energetically to receive what's coming.

Ready to discover how your zodiac sign works with the Fire Horse? Turn to Chapter 5.

CHAPTER FIVE

Your Zodiac Sign and the Fire Horse

"My sign carries ancient wisdom. I honor my nature as I walk into this powerful year with awareness and grace."

Not all zodiac signs experience the Fire Horse year the same way.

Some signs will feel empowered, energized, and ready to leap. Others will feel pushed, challenged, or overwhelmed by the speed of change.

Understanding how your sign interacts with the Horse helps you prepare for what's coming and gives you tools to work with the energy rather than against it.

How to Find Your Chinese Zodiac Sign

Your Chinese zodiac sign is determined by your birth year, not your birth month.

Here's the quick guide:

Year	Zodiac Sign	Start Date	End Date	Characteristics
1950	Tiger	Feb 17 1950	Feb 05 1951	Bold, passionate, charismatic; can be impulsive.
1951	Rabbit	Feb 06 1951	Jan 26 1952	Gentle, artistic, diplomatic; avoids conflict.
1952	Dragon	Jan 27 1952	Feb 13 1953	Confident, visionary, influential; may expect perfection.
1953	Snake	Feb 14 1953	Feb 02 1954	Wise, intuitive, elegant; sometimes overly cautious.

Year	Animal	Start	End	Traits
1954	Horse	Feb 03 1954	Jan 23 1955	Independent, energetic, expressive; can feel trapped.
1955	Goat	Jan 24 1955	Feb 11 1956	Compassionate, creative, nurturing, sensitive to pressure.
1956	Monkey	Feb 12 1956	Jan 30 1957	Inventive, witty, playful; may become scattered.
1957	Rooster	Jan 31 1957	Feb 17 1958	Organized, honest, hardworking; can be critical.
1958	Dog	Feb 18 1958	Feb 07 1959	Loyal, protective, caring; carries emotional burdens.
1959	Pig	Feb 08 1959	Jan 27 1960	Warm, generous, joyful; may be too trusting.
1960	Rat	Jan 28 1960	Feb 14 1961	Clever, intuitive, resourceful; prone to overthinking.
1961	Ox	Feb 15 1961	Feb 04 1962	Patient, grounded, reliable; may resist change.

1962	Tiger	Feb 05 1962	Jan 24 1963	Bold, passionate, charismatic; can be impulsive.
1963	Rabbit	Jan 25 1963	Feb 12 1964	Gentle, artistic, diplomatic; avoids conflict.
1964	Dragon	Feb 13 1964	Feb 01 1965	Confident, visionary, influential; may expect perfection.
1965	Snake	Feb 02 1965	Feb 20 1966	Wise, intuitive, elegant; sometimes overly cautious.
1966	Horse	Jan 21 1966	Feb 08 1967	Independent, energetic, expressive; can feel trapped.
1967	Goat	Feb 09 1967	Jan 29 1968	Compassionate, creative, nurturing; sensitive to pressure.
1968	Monkey	Jan 30 1968	Feb 16 1969	Inventive, witty, playful; may become scattered.
1969	Rooster	Feb 17 1969	Feb 05 1970	Organized, honest, hardworking; can be critical.

1970	Dog	Feb 06 1970	Jan 26 1971	Loyal, protective, caring; carries emotional burdens.
1971	Pig	Jan 27 1971	Feb 14 1972	Warm, generous, joyful; may be too trusting.
1972	Rat	Feb 15 1972	Feb 02 1973	Clever, intuitive, resourceful; prone to overthinking.
1973	Ox	Feb 03 1973	Jan 22 1974	Patient, grounded, reliable; may resist change.
1974	Tiger	Jan 23 1974	Feb 10 1975	Bold, passionate, charismatic; can be impulsive.
1975	Rabbit	Feb 11 1975	Jan 30 1976	Gentle, artistic, diplomatic; avoids conflict.
1976	Dragon	Jan 31 1976	Feb 17 1977	Confident, visionary, influential; may expect perfection.
1977	Snake	Feb 18 1977	Feb 06 1978	Wise, intuitive, elegant; sometimes overly cautious.

1978	Horse	Feb 07 1978	Jan 27 1979	Independent, energetic, expressive; can feel trapped.
1979	Goat	Jan 28 1979	Feb 15 1980	Compassionate, creative, nurturing; sensitive to pressure.
1980	Monkey	Feb 16 1980	Feb 04 1981	Inventive, witty, playful; may become scattered.
1981	Rooster	Feb 05 1981	Jan 24 1982	Organized, honest, hardworking; can be critical.
1982	Dog	Jan 25 1982	Feb 12 1983	Loyal, protective, caring; carries emotional burdens.
1983	Pig	Feb 13 1983	Feb 01 1984	Warm, generous, joyful; may be too trusting.
1984	Rat	Feb 02 1984	Feb 19 1985	Clever, intuitive, resourceful; prone to overthinking.
1985	Ox	Feb 20 1985	Feb 08 1986	Patient, grounded, reliable; may resist change.

Year	Animal	Start Date	End Date	Traits
1986	Tiger	Feb 09 1986	Jan 28 1987	Bold, passionate, charismatic; can be impulsive.
1987	Rabbit	Jan 29 1987	Feb 16 1988	Gentle, artistic, diplomatic; avoids conflict.
1988	Dragon	Feb 17 1988	Feb 05 1989	Confident, visionary, influential; may expect perfection.
1989	Snake	Feb 06 1989	Jan 26 1990	Wise, intuitive, elegant; sometimes overly cautious.
1990	Horse	Jan 27 1990	Feb 14 1991	Independent, energetic, expressive; can feel trapped.
1991	Goat	Feb 15 1991	Feb 03 1992	Compassionate, creative, nurturing; sensitive to pressure.
1992	Monkey	Feb 04 1992	Jan 22 1993	Inventive, witty, playful; may become scattered.
1993	Rooster	Jan 23 1993	Feb 09 1994	Organized, honest, hardworking; can be critical.

Year	Animal	Start	End	Traits
1994	Dog	Feb 10 1994	Jan 30 1995	Loyal, protective, caring; carries emotional burdens.
1995	Pig	Jan 31 1995	Feb 18 1996	Warm, generous, joyful; may be too trusting.
1996	Rat	Feb 19 1996	Feb 06 1997	Clever, intuitive, resourceful; prone to overthinking.
1997	Ox	Feb 07 1997	Jan 27 1998	Patient, grounded, reliable; may resist change.
1998	Tiger	Jan 28 1998	Feb 15 1999	Bold, passionate, charismatic; can be impulsive.
1999	Rabbit	Feb 16 1999	Feb 04 2000	Gentle, artistic, diplomatic; avoids conflict.
2000	Dragon	Feb 05 2000	Jan 23 2001	Confident, visionary, influential; may expect perfection.
2001	Snake	Jan 24 2001	Feb 11 2002	Wise, intuitive, elegant; sometimes overly cautious.

2002	Horse	Feb 12 2002	Jan 31 2003	Independent, energetic, expressive; can feel trapped.
2003	Goat	Feb 01 2003	Jan 21 2004	Compassionate, creative, nurturing; sensitive to pressure.
2004	Monkey	Jan 22 2004	Feb 08 2005	Inventive, witty, playful; may become scattered.
2005	Rooster	Feb 09 2005	Jan 28 2006	Organized, honest, hardworking; can be critical.
2006	Dog	Jan 29 2006	Feb 17 2007	Loyal, protective, caring; carries emotional burdens.
2007	Pig	Feb 18 2007	Feb 06 2008	Warm, generous, joyful; may be too trusting.
2008	Rat	Feb 07 2008	Jan 25 2009	Clever, intuitive, resourceful; prone to overthinking.
2009	Ox	Jan 26 2009	Feb 13 2010	Patient, grounded, reliable; may resist change.

2010	Tiger	Feb 14 2010	Feb 02 2011	Bold, passionate, charismatic; can be impulsive.
2011	Rabbit	Feb 03 2011	Jan 22 2012	Gentle, artistic, diplomatic; avoids conflict.
2012	Dragon	Jan 23 2012	Feb 09 2013	Confident, visionary, influential; may expect perfection.
2013	Snake	Feb 10 2013	Jan 30 2014	Wise, intuitive, elegant; sometimes overly cautious.
2014	Horse	Jan 31 2014	Feb 18 2015	Independent, energetic, expressive; can feel trapped.
2015	Goat	Feb 19 2015	Feb 07 2016	Compassionate, creative, nurturing; sensitive to pressure.
2016	Monkey	Feb 08 2016	Jan 27 2017	Inventive, witty, playful; may become scattered.
2017	Rooster	Jan 28 2017	Feb 15 2018	Organized, honest, hardworking; can be critical.

Year	Animal	Start	End	Traits
2018	Dog	Feb 16 2018	Feb 04 2019	Loyal, protective, caring; carries emotional burdens.
2019	Pig	Feb 05 2019	Jan 24 2020	Warm, generous, joyful; may be too trusting.
2020	Rat	Jan 25 2020	Feb 11 2021	Clever, intuitive, resourceful; prone to overthinking.
2021	Ox	Feb 12 2021	Jan 31 2022	Patient, grounded, reliable; may resist change.
2022	Tiger	Feb 01 2022	Jan 21 2023	Bold, passionate, charismatic; can be impulsive.
2023	Rabbit	Jan 22 2023	Feb 09 2024	Gentle, artistic, diplomatic; avoids conflict.
2024	Dragon	Feb 10 2024	Jan 28 2025	Confident, visionary, influential; may expect perfection.
2025	Snake	Jan 29 2025	Feb 16 2026	Wise, intuitive, elegant; sometimes overly cautious.

2026	Horse	Feb 17 2026	Feb 05 2027	Independent, energetic, expressive; can feel trapped.

THE HORSE AND ITS RELATIONSHIP WITH OTHER SIGNS

The Horse is one of the most independent, spirited, and fast-paced signs in the Chinese zodiac.

Governed by movement, passion, and freedom, the Horse thrives in environments where energy flows, ideas expand, and intuition is trusted.

But the way a Fire Horse year influences each zodiac sign varies greatly. Understanding these relationships helps you prepare for the Fire Horse energy and align your expectations with the natural rhythms of the year.

HORSE + TIGER, GOAT, AND DOG: NATURAL ALLIES

If you're a Tiger, Goat, or Dog, 2026 is your year.

These are the Horse's closest allies. The energy flows naturally, and you'll feel supported by the Fire Horse momentum.

Tiger brings bravery and vision, helping the Horse focus its wild energy with purpose. In a Fire Horse year, Tiger individuals may feel especially empowered—ready to take bold steps. This is your time to lead, launch, and leap.

Goat (Sheep) harmonizes with the Horse's creative spirit, softening the intensity and offering emotional comfort. The year supports artistic projects, heart-centered work, and self-expression for Goats. Trust your intuition and follow your creative impulses.

The Dog shares the Horse's enthusiasm and loyalty. Dogs find grounding in the Horse's passion, while the Horse benefits from the Dog's steadiness. This year brings opportunities for mutual support, healthy relationships, and renewed motivation. Stay open to collaboration.

HORSE + RAT: OPPOSING ENERGIES

If you're a Rat, 2026 will feel challenging.

The Horse and the Rat sit directly opposite each other in the zodiac, creating tension and mismatched priorities.

Rats thrive on planning, security, and careful strategy, while the Fire Horse charges ahead with instinct and speed.

In 2026, Rats may feel pushed, rushed, or overwhelmed by the fast-moving energy. Your natural tendency to think things through will clash with the Horse's impulsive momentum.

What to do:
Ground yourself. Create stable routines. Keep calm spaces at home. Don't fight the speed, just make sure you have a safe place to land when things move too fast.

Focus on what you can control. Let go of what you can't.

HORSE + OX AND ROOSTER: CHALLENGING BUT TRANSFORMATIVE

If you're an Ox or Rooster, 2026 will push you out of your comfort zone.

Ox and Rooster work hard, follow structure, and prefer predictability. The Fire Horse brings unpredictability, spontaneity, and heat.

This contrast may feel uncomfortable at first, but it creates tremendous space for growth.

Ox: You like slow, steady progress. The Fire Horse doesn't. But if you stay flexible and open-minded, the year can bring breakthroughs, new confidence, and long-awaited changes. Don't resist. Adapt.

Rooster: You thrive on order and precision. The Fire Horse thrives on instinct. This year will test your ability to trust the process without needing to control every detail. Let go a little. The results might surprise you.

HORSE + MONKEY: EXCITING BUT UNSTABLE

If you're a Monkey, 2026 will be a wild ride.

The Horse and the Monkey share curiosity and enthusiasm, but their energies can create chaos when amplified.

Monkeys may experience 2026 as a year of big ideas, sudden shifts, and unpredictable opportunities. Your mind will race. Your options will multiply. You'll feel pulled in ten directions at once.

What to do:
Create order. Write things down. Prioritize ruthlessly. Otherwise, the Fire Horse energy will spread you too thin, and you'll burn out before the year is halfway through.

Focus on one or two big goals. Let the rest go.

HORSE + RABBIT, PIG, AND SNAKE: SOFT HARMONIZERS

If you're a Rabbit, Pig, or Snake, 2026 will move fast—but you can handle it.

These signs do not naturally clash with the Horse, but they move more gently through life.

Rabbit values peace and may find the year intense, but you can benefit from adopting a more courageous mindset. Step out of your comfort zone. The Fire Horse will support you if you're willing to be brave.

Pig thrives in supportive environments and may find new sources of joy if you follow your intuition. Trust your gut. Say yes to what feels good. Let go of what doesn't.

Snake brings wisdom and depth, helping to balance the Horse's impulsiveness with insight. Your year will be guided by inner transformation rather than external speed. Go inward. Reflect. Trust the process.

HORSE + DRAGON: DYNAMIC POWER PAIR

If you're a Dragon, 2026 is explosive.

The Dragon and the Horse both carry strong yang energy.

When aligned, they create unstoppable momentum, leadership, breakthroughs, new ventures, and bold achievements.

But if either sign is emotionally unbalanced, the combination sparks conflict, stubbornness, and pride.

What to do:
Stay humble. Stay emotionally clear. If you can manage your ego and keep your heart open, 2026 will be one of the most powerful years of your life.

But if you let pride take over, the Fire Horse will humble you fast.

HORSE + HORSE: DOUBLE FIRE

If you're a Horse, this is your year—but it's also your test.

A Fire Horse year for a Horse person is like standing in front of a mirror that magnifies everything.

Your strengths will shine brighter. Your weaknesses will show up louder.

If you're aligned, grounded, and clear, 2026 will feel like flying.

If you're scattered, unbalanced, or avoiding your truth, the year will force you to face it.

What to do:

Prepare. Ground yourself. Clear your energy. Do the work in this guide.

This is your year to rise—but only if you're ready.

THE ONE THING EVERYONE SHOULD DO

If you do nothing else this year, do this one thing—because it is incredibly powerful:

ACTION 29: CARRY OR DISPLAY A SMALL SHEEP (GOAT) FIGURINE.

In Chinese astrology, the Sheep is the Horse's secret friend, its quiet protector, its harmonizer, its calming force.

During a Fire Horse year, this energy becomes even more important. A small Sheep symbol can soften intensity, dissolve conflict, and stabilize the fast-moving energy around you.

Keep a tiny Sheep in your wallet or purse, place one on your desk facing your personal success direction, or even tuck it discreetly inside your bra.

Wherever you keep it, this gentle companion helps balance the fiery momentum of 2026 and brings in steadiness, clarity, and good fortune.

You now understand how your sign works with the Fire Horse.

Some of you will flow. Some of you will fight. Some of you will fly.

But all of you can prepare. And preparation is what makes the difference between surviving the Fire Horse year and thriving in it.

CHAPTER SIX

The Power of Three: Focus, Heal, Rise

"When I focus, I become unstoppable. When I heal, I become whole.
When I rise, I transform everything."

You've assessed all nine areas of your life. You know where you stand.

Now it's time to create your action plan, a focused, strategic approach that will carry you from where you are today to where you want to be on February 17, 2026.

This isn't about doing everything. It's about doing the right things.

The Fire Horse rewards focus and clarity. It punishes scattered energy and half-finished efforts.

So here's what we're going to do:

You've assessed all nine areas of your life. You know where you stand.

Now it's time to create your action plan, a focused, strategic approach that will carry you from where you are today to where you want to be during the year of the Fire Horse that ends in February 2027.

This isn't about doing everything. It's about doing the *right* things.

The Fire Horse rewards focus and clarity. It punishes scattered energy and half-finished efforts.

So, here's what we're going to do:

Step 1: Identify Your Three Critical Areas

Look back at your assessments from Chapter 3. Which three areas are challenges **right now** that could get **worse** if left unaddressed?

These are the areas that keep you up at night. The ones that drain your energy. The ones you've been avoiding or "managing" instead of truly healing.

Remember: The Fire Horse magnifies everything. What feels like a small problem today will feel like a crisis in 2026 if you don't address it now.

On a piece of paper, write down your three critical areas:

Critical Area #1: _____

Critical Area #2: _____

Critical Area #3: _____

Don't overthink this. Your gut knows which areas need the most attention.

Trust your instinct.

Step 2: Answer the Questions for Each Area

For each of your three critical areas, return to Chapter 3 and answer the assessment questions on paper. Write them out by hand. Don't just think about them, actually write the answers down on paper.

Writing clarifies your thoughts. It brings unconscious feelings to the surface. It creates accountability.

For each critical area, ask yourself:

- What is the current state of this area in my life?
- What will happen (or is happening) if I don't address this before February 17, 2026?
- What would my life look like if this area were strong, clear, and aligned?
- What specific actions from Chapter 3 will I commit to completing?

Be honest. Be thorough. This is your foundation.

Step 3: Complete Your Three Critical Areas by February 16, 2026, or as soon as you get this book

Now that you know your three areas and have written your answers, it's time to take action.

Your goal is to complete the recommended actions for all three critical areas **before February 16, 2026**, the day before the Fire Horse year officially begins. **This is your sacred window. Use it wisely.**

If you got the book later, commit to completing it as soon as possible.

A FLOW THAT SUPPORTS YOUR HIGHEST WORK:

Phase 1: Immediate Action (First 30 days)

Start with the quick wins, the actions that can be completed in a day or a week. These create momentum and give you confidence.

Examples:

- Answer the questions from the three critical areas
- Clear clutter under your bed
- Schedule health appointments
- Hang a wind chime
- Place coins in your Wealth corner
- Write your gratitude lists

Phase 2: Deep Work (First 60 days)

Tackle the harder actions, the ones that require emotional work, difficult conversations, or sustained effort.

Examples:

- Make emotional amends with family
- Face your financial reality
- Heal your current job (or find a new one)
- Create your love altar and reset your bedroom
- Start your daily spiritual practice

Phase 3: Final Integration (First 90 days)

Review your work. Make any final adjustments. Ensure everything is complete and aligned.

Walk through your home and feel the shift in energy.

Take a deep breath. You're ready.

Step 4: Work on Two Areas at a Time Going Forward

Once your three critical areas are complete, you have six remaining areas from the Bagua to address. Just work on **two areas at a time**.

This keeps you focused without overwhelming you.

Here's how:

1. Choose two of your remaining six areas.
2. Return to Chapter 3 and complete the recommended actions for both areas.
3. Give yourself 30-45 days to complete both areas.
4. Once complete, choose the next two areas and repeat.

Your goal is to be friends with the Fire Horse as soon as possible, but give you the space to complete it by late Spring/early Summer 2026; all nine areas of your life will be aligned, clear, and strong.

And you'll be riding the Fire Horse with grace, power, and confidence.

A WORD OF ENCOURAGEMENT

This plan might feel overwhelming at first. You might look at your three critical areas and think, "I can't do this."

But here's the truth: **You *can* do this!**

You don't have to be perfect. You just have to be willing.

Every small action you take shifts your energy. Every question you answer brings clarity. Every area you heal opens a door.

The Fire Horse doesn't ask for perfection. It asks for alignment. For honesty. For courage.

And those qualities are already inside you.

You picked up this guide because you're ready. Trust that.

Do the work. Take it one step at a time. And remember:

THE FIRE HORSE REWARDS THOSE WHO SHOW UP PREPARED.

Ready to discover the powerful rituals for welcoming the Fire Horse? Turn to Chapter 7.

CHAPTER SEVEN

Rituals for Welcoming the Fire Horse Energy

"With every ritual, I call in clarity, protection, and momentum. I am blessed, guided, and ready."

You've done the work.

You've assessed your life. You've cleared the clutter. You've faced what needs healing. You've aligned your energy with your goals.

Or maybe you're reading this during the Fire Horse year itself, and you're ready to jump in right now.

Either way, you're here. And that's what matters.

ABOUT TIMING AND COMMITMENT

Ideally, you'll complete your preparations before February 16, 2026—the day before the Fire Horse year officially begins.

But life happens.

Maybe you didn't finish everything in time. Maybe you're getting this book in March, or June, or October of 2026.

Here's what you need to know:

THE FIRE HORSE HONORS COMMITMENT.

It doesn't matter if you start on February 17 or July 20. What matters is that you *start*. What matters is your intention. What matters is your willingness to show up and do the work.

If you're reading this during the Fire Horse year, follow the same process:

1. Identify your three critical areas.

2. Answer the assessment questions for each.

3. Complete the recommended actions from Chapter 3.

4. Then work on two areas at a time for the remaining six.

The energy responds to your commitment, not to perfect timing.

Start where you are. The Fire Horse will meet you there.

ABOUT THESE RITUALS

This chapter shares traditional Chinese rituals for welcoming the Lunar New Year and honoring the Fire Horse's arrival. But here's the fact: **These rituals are completely optional.**

You don't have to do any of them to have a powerful Fire Horse year.

The work you've already done in Chapters 3-5, clearing your space, facing your challenges, aligning your energy, that's what creates transformation. That's what prepares you.

These rituals are simply *invitations.* They are beautiful, meaningful ways to mark the transition and set intention. I use some of them, especially #1, #3, #4, #6, and #15, a few times a year.

If a ritual speaks to you, if it feels right in your body, if it lights something up inside you, then do it.

If it doesn't resonate, skip it. No guilt. No judgment. Trust yourself.

It's all about intention.

A ritual performed with genuine intention and an open heart is powerful, no matter how simple.

A ritual performed out of obligation or fear carries no energy at all.

So read through these rituals. Feel into them. Choose what calls to you. And let the rest go.

THE WEEK BEFORE: FEBRUARY 10-16, 2026

If you're reading this before the Fire Horse year begins, this week is your final preparation. If you're reading this later, you can still do these rituals anytime to refresh your energy and create a sense of renewal.

RITUAL 1: THE GREAT CLEARING

In Chinese tradition, you clean your home thoroughly before the new year to sweep away bad luck and make room for good fortune, just as Westerners do before New Year's.

What to do:

- Deep clean your home from top to bottom, from the back to the front, especially your entryway, bedroom, and any Bagua areas you've been working on.

- Open all windows for at least 15 minutes to let fresh air circulate.

- Wash your front door (inside and out) to welcome new opportunities.

- Remove any dead plants, burned-out light bulbs, or broken items.

- Vacuum or sweep from the back of your home toward the front doors, symbolically pushing out old energy.

As you clean, say silently or aloud: "I release all that no longer serves me. I make space for blessings, abundance, and joy."

RITUAL 2: PAY YOUR DEBTS AND CLEAR YOUR SLATE

Before the new year begins (or whenever you're starting fresh), settle what you can. This creates energetic freedom and prevents carrying old burdens forward.

What to do:

- Pay off any small debts if possible. Make payment arrangements.

- Return borrowed items.

- Apologize to anyone you may have hurt (even if it's just in your heart).

- Forgive anyone who hurt you. This is not for them; it is to free yourself.

You don't need perfection. You just need intention.

RITUAL 3: PREPARE YOUR SACRED SPACE OR ALTAR

Create a small sacred space or altar somewhere in your home to honor the Fire Horse year. This becomes your anchor point—a place to set intentions, express gratitude, and reconnect with your goals throughout the year.

This doesn't have to be elaborate. It can be as simple as a cleared area on top of your dresser, a bookshelf, a small table, or even a corner of your desk.

What to include:

- A red cloth or scarf (red activates Fire energy and wards off negativity)

- A small Horse figurine (any color, but gold or red is ideal)

- A Sheep figurine (the Horse's secret friend for balance and support)

- Fresh flowers or a living plant

- A candle (red, orange, or gold for Fire energy)

- A bowl of fresh water (to balance the Fire)

- Written intentions for 2026 (see Ritual 5)

Place your sacred space in a clean, elevated area, never on the floor. The Recognition area (back center of your home) or the Wealth area (back left) are ideal locations, but anywhere that feels right to you works beautifully.

Remember: This is *your* sacred space. Include only what speaks to your heart.

PS: If you are a Fire Horse as I am, I recommend that you have at least a small figurine displayed in your bedroom or somewhere in your house.

RITUAL 4: THE GRATITUDE RELEASE

February 16, 2026: The Day Before (Or Your Personal Start Date), this is a day of release, gratitude, and intention-setting.

Take time to honor what's ending. Even if the past year was difficult, it taught you something. Even if it was painful, it shaped you.

What to do:

5. Write a letter to the past. Thank it for what it gave you (the lessons, the growth, the challenges, the blessings).

6. Write down anything you're ready to release (old stories, limiting beliefs, past hurts, regrets, fears).

7. Safely burn the letter (in a fireproof container or fireplace) or tear it up and throw it away. As you do, say: "I release what no longer serves me. I am free."

This clears space for what's coming.

Ps. I also use this ritual at the end of the calendar year, when I need to change my energy, or when I conduct retreats.

RITUAL 5: WRITE YOUR FIRE HORSE INTENTIONS

Now that you've released the old, it's time to call in the new.

What to do:

On a beautiful piece of paper (or in a special journal), write your intentions for the Fire Horse year.

Don't write vague wishes. Write clear, powerful statements in the present tense, as if they're already true:

- "I am healthy, strong, and full of energy."

- "My career is aligned with my purpose, and I am financially abundant."

- "My relationships are loving, supportive, and joyful."

- "I trust myself and move through life with courage and grace."

Write as many as you want, but make sure each one feels *true* in your body when you read it. For financial goals, avoid writing a number down. It's best to use words like abundance, prosperity, and unexpected amounts so you don't block the money from coming in.

Place this paper in your sacred space or somewhere you'll see it daily. Please don't share or talk about it with anyone. This brings in the ego, which can delay things for you.

RITUAL 6: TAKE A CLEANSING BATH OR SHOWER

Water purifies. It washes away old energy and prepares you for the new.

What to do:

Take a ritual bath or shower with intention.

If taking a bath:

- Add sea salt (purification)

- Add essential oils like lavender, rosemary, or eucalyptus

- Light candles

- Play soft music

If taking a shower:

Visualize the water washing away everything you're releasing.

- Use a special soap or body scrub that smells uplifting.

- Stand under the water and say: "I am cleansed. I am renewed. I am ready."

After you dry off, put on something fresh and comfortable.

February 17, 2026: The Fire Horse Arrives (Or Your Fresh Start Day)

This is the day the Fire Horse officially takes the reins, or the day you commit to your fresh start.

How you spend this day (or your chosen start date) sets an energetic tone. Approach it with joy, reverence, and intention.

RITUAL 7: WEAR RED

In Chinese tradition, red symbolizes good luck, protection, and vitality. Wearing red on the Lunar New Year invites blessings and wards off negativity.

It doesn't have to be a full outfit—red underwear, socks, a scarf, jewelry, or even a hair tie works.

Just make sure you're wearing *something* red.

RITUAL 8: EAT LUCKY FOODS

Food carries symbolism and energy. On Lunar New Year, certain foods invite prosperity, longevity, and good fortune.

Traditional lucky foods:

- Dumplings (wealth—shaped like ancient gold ingots)

- Long noodles (longevity—don't cut them!)

- Fish (abundance and prosperity)

- Oranges and tangerines (good luck and happiness)

- Spring rolls (wealth—shaped like gold bars)

- Sweet rice balls (family togetherness)

You don't have to cook a feast. Even one or two symbolic foods will do.

As you eat, say silently: "I welcome abundance, health, and joy into my life."

RITUAL 9: LIGHT YOUR CANDLE AND SET YOUR INTENTION

If possible, greet the sunrise of your fresh start day. If not, any time during the day works.

What to do:

8. Stand near a window or step outside.

9. Take three deep breaths.

10. Say aloud or silently: "I welcome the Fire Horse with gratitude and courage. I am aligned, grounded, and ready. This is my year."

11. Go to your sacred space and light the candle.

12. Read your written intentions aloud.

13. Sit quietly for a few moments and feel the energy of this new beginning.

This simple act anchors your intentions into reality.

Ritual 10: Create a Positive Day

In Chinese tradition, how you spend the first day of the new year sets the tone for the entire year. I am not Chinese or Buddhist, but this ritual is universal.

On this day, if you can:

- Avoid arguing or complaining

- Focus on joy, kindness, and gratitude

- Spend time with people you love

- Do things that bring you joy

- Rest and celebrate

Set the energetic tone you want for your entire year.

Ritual 11: Give and Receive (Optional)

In Chinese tradition, red envelopes (hongbao) filled with money are given as blessings, especially to children, unmarried adults, and elders.

If this appeals to you, you can adapt this ritual to invite abundance:

- Place a small amount of money in a red envelope.

- Give it to someone you love with a blessing: "May this year bring you joy and prosperity."

- If you receive a red envelope, accept it with both hands and gratitude.

- Tip a little more than usual.

This activates the flow of giving and receiving—essential for abundance.

Moving Forward: The First Two Weeks and Beyond

The first 15 days after your start date are especially powerful for building momentum.

RITUAL 12: CONNECT WITH OTHERS

Connection strengthens energy. Make time to see the people who matter to you during the first two weeks.

Even a phone call, video chat, or thoughtful message counts.

RITUAL 13: KEEP YOUR SACRED SPACE ACTIVE

Your sacred space isn't a one-day decoration. It's a living, energetic anchor.

What to do:

- Light your candle daily or weekly (even for just a minute).

- Refresh the flowers or water regularly.

- Read your intentions aloud once a week.

- Add new items as the year unfolds, such as photos of achievements, symbols of blessings, and gratitude notes.

This keeps your energy aligned with what you're calling in.

RITUAL 14: EXPRESS GRATITUDE DAILY

Gratitude is the fastest way to raise your vibration and align with abundance.

Every morning or evening, write down three things you're grateful for.

They don't have to be big. A warm cup of coffee. A kind word from a friend. The sun on your face.

Gratitude tells the universe, "I see the blessings. I'm ready for more."

RITUAL 15: TRACING THE NINE STARS (FOR CLEARING HEAVY ENERGY)

If 2025 was a difficult year, marked by depression, financial or health challenges, conflict, or a lingering heaviness, this ancient Feng Shui ritual can help clear stagnant energy from your home and uplift the vibration of everyone who lives there. You can perform it at any time of the year. Still, if you've experienced serious illness, a major financial setback, or the end of a relationship or marriage, I recommend doing it as soon as possible.

You can also do it multiple times a year when you need a major shift in your life. Just don't overdo it, as you may invoke the energy of desperation. If you do it every month, you are expecting it not to work and don't have the patience to allow it to work for you.

I like to do it before I move into a house, when I sense the energy is sluggish (you will know when you return for a vacation and struggle to take action in your life), or after a major illness of one of the residents.

Nine-Star Tracing: Step-by-Step Guide

Start by cleaning and organizing your home. The Nine Star Tracing is a deeper energy-clearing practice that uses the **Three Secrets Reinforcement** (body, mind, and spirit). The Nine-Star Tracing is a sacred method that activates each of the nine life areas with intention, gesture, and mantra. Follow the steps below to clear the old and prepare your home for new blessings.

Step 1 – Clean the physical space

Before any energetic work, tidy the room. Remove clutter, dust, and anything broken. A clean space allows the Chi to move freely and supports the clearing you're about to do.

Step 2 – Set your overall intention

Stand in the center of the room and take a few deep breaths.

Choose a simple intention, such as:

"I am clearing old energy and activating harmony, protection, and good fortune in this space."

This prepares your energy field and aligns your mind with the work ahead.

Step 3 – Prepare the Three Secrets (Body, Mind, Spirit)

Body — Ousting Mudra

You'll use the **Ousting Mudra**, a traditional hand gesture used to eliminate unwanted or stagnant energy.

You will flick your fingers.
(See the picture for the correct hand position.)

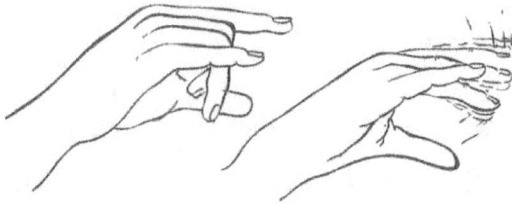

Mind — Focus on the outcome

Before you walk the nine-star path, locate each of the areas of the home. You can do it for each floor, the main floor only, or a room. Decide what outcome you want for each of the nine life areas (health, career, knowledge, family, wealth, recognition, relationships, creativity, helpful people) or just the overall feeling. Hold one outcome in mind for each point of the star.

Spirit — Heart Sutra Mantra

At each point of the star, you'll repeat the Heart Sutra Mantra **nine times:**

"GATE GATE,
BORO GATE,
BORO SUN GATE,
BODHI SO PO HE."
(*Gate is pronounced Gat-ay.*)

This mantra acts like a prayer, loosely translated as **"may obstacles fall away and may our wishes be granted."**

Step 4 – Clarify your nine intentions.

Choose one focused outcome for each of the nine life areas:

1. **Health** – strength, vitality, healing
2. **Career** – direction, clarity, opportunities
3. **Knowledge/Spirituality** – insight, wisdom
4. **Family** – harmony, understanding
5. **Finance** – flow, abundance
6. **Recognition** – confidence, visibility

7. **Relationships** – love, compassion

8. **Creativity** – inspiration, joy

9. **Helpful People/Travel** – support, divine timing, safe travels

Keep your intentions simple and sincere.

Step 5 – Begin at the first point of the Nine-Star Path

Go to the first point in your nine-star diagram.

Hold the **Ousting Mudra,** think of your intention for that life area, and recite the mantra. Start at point 1 and follow the stops as traced below:

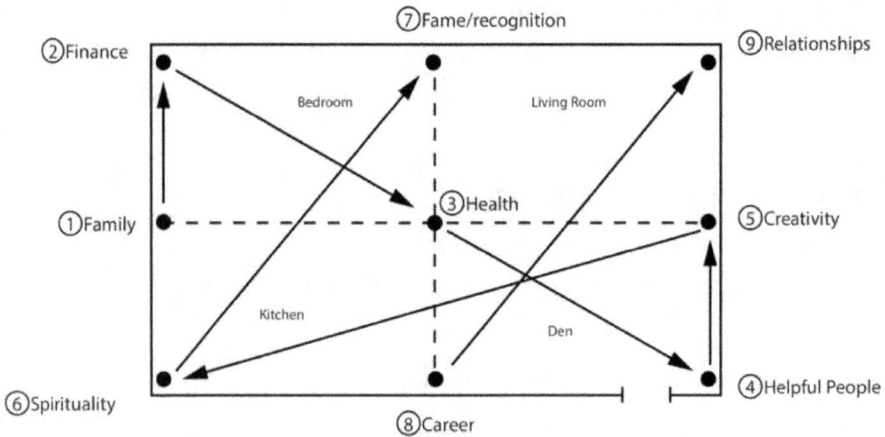

Step 6 – Activate each point

At **every** point of the star:

1. Hold the **Ousting Mudra** (body).
2. Focus on the outcome for that life area (mind).
3. Recite the mantra **nine times** (spirit).

Feel the old energy dissolving and the new energy settling into place.

Step 7 – Walk through all nine points

Move through the nine-star pattern in sequence.
At each point, repeat the same process:
Mudra + Intention + Mantra.

This alignment of **body, mind, and spirit** is what makes the clearing so profound.

Step 8 – Seal the practice

Return to the center of the room.
Place your hands over your heart and say silently:

"This clearing is complete.

May this space support my highest good and the highest good of all who enter."

This seals the energy and anchors the intention.

Step 9 – Notice the shift

Spend a moment in the room.

You may feel lighter, calmer, or more grounded.

This is your space responding to the clearing—open, receptive, and ready for what's next. You will feel the difference immediately.

A FINAL WORD ON RITUALS

Rituals work because they anchor intention into action.

They don't have to be perfect. They don't have to be elaborate. They just have to be *sincere.*

Choose the rituals that speak to your heart. Adapt them to fit your life. Trust that your intention is enough.

The Fire Horse doesn't ask for perfection. It asks for presence. For respect. For courage. And you already have all three.

You've prepared. You've aligned. You've honored the transition.

Now it's time to step into your power.

The Fire Horse is ready. Are you?

Ready for the final chapter? Turn to Chapter 8 for closing wisdom and your path forward.

CHAPTER EIGHT

Final Words: You Are Ready?

"I step into 2026 prepared, empowered, and aligned. The Fire Horse carries me toward my highest destiny."

You've come to the end of this guide.

But you haven't come to the end of your journey.

In fact, you're standing at the beginning of something extraordinary.

The Fire Horse year isn't just another year on the calendar. It's an invitation. A doorway. A once-in-a-lifetime opportunity to step into the fullest, most powerful version of yourself.

And you're ready for it.

What You've Accomplished

Let's pause for a moment and acknowledge what you've done.

You learned about the Fire Horse energy—its intensity, its power, its gifts.

You mapped your life using the ancient Bagua, seeing clearly which areas need your attention.

You assessed all nine areas of your life with honesty and courage.

You discovered how your Chinese zodiac sign interacts with the Horse, and you learned the secret of the Sheep as your ally.

You created a strategic action plan—identifying your three critical areas and committing to working through them before moving forward.

You explored powerful rituals for welcoming the Fire Horse with intention and grace.

This is *not* small work.

This is the kind of preparation that changes everything.

THE TRUTH ABOUT TRANSFORMATION

Here's something most people don't understand about powerful years like this:

The Fire Horse doesn't *give* you anything you don't already have.

It *reveals* what was always there.

Your courage. Your strength. Your clarity. Your worthiness.

These qualities were inside you all along.

The Fire Horse year simply magnifies them. It gives you permission to stop hiding. To stop playing small. To stop waiting for the "right time" because *this* is the right time.

When you align yourself, when you clear the clutter, heal the wounds, and set strong intentions, you create space for this energy to work *with* you, not against you.

And that's what preparation is really about.

Not perfection. Not control. Alignment.

WHAT TO EXPECT IN A FIRE HORSE YEAR

Let me be honest with you. 2026 will not be a gentle year.

It will be fast. It will be intense. It will push you. But if you've done the work, if you've prepared yourself, you won't be overwhelmed by it.

You'll feel challenged, yes. But you'll also feel *alive*.

You'll experience breakthrough moments, those sudden shifts where something you've been working toward for years finally clicks into place.

You'll attract opportunities that seem to come out of nowhere.

You'll find yourself saying yes to things you would have been too afraid to try before.

You'll discover reserves of courage and resilience you didn't know you had.

And at the end of the year, when you look back, you'll barely recognize the person you were on February 17.

That's the gift of the Fire Horse.

It doesn't let you stay the same.

WHEN THINGS GET HARD

There will be moments during the Fire Horse year when you feel overwhelmed.

When the pace feels too fast.

When old patterns resurface.

When you doubt yourself.

When those moments come, remember this:

You are not being tested. You are being strengthened.

The Fire Horse doesn't push you to break you. It pushes you to *reveal* yourself.

When things get hard, come back to your sacred space. Light your candle. Reread your intentions. Remind yourself why you started this journey.

And if you need to, go back to Chapter 3. Reassess. Adjust. Realign.

This guide isn't meant to be read once and put away. It's a living tool. Use it throughout the year whenever you need grounding, clarity, or a reminder of your power.

TRUST THE PROCESS

One of the hardest lessons of a Fire Horse year is learning to trust the process even when you can't see the outcome.

The Fire Horse moves fast. Things will happen quickly, sometimes too quickly for your logical mind to keep up.

Doors will open. Doors will close.

People will enter your life. People will leave.

Opportunities will appear out of nowhere.

Plans you thought were solid will shift.

And through it all, you'll be asked to trust.

Trust that you're being guided.

Trust that what's leaving needed to go.

Trust that what's arriving is meant for you.

Trust that even when things feel chaotic, there's an intelligence at work far greater than your ability to control.

The Fire Horse asks you to surrender the illusion of control and step into the power of *flow*.

THE YEAR AFTER

On February 3, 2027, the Fire Horse year will end.

The Fire Sheep will arrive, and the energy will shift again, this time into something softer, more creative, more harmonious.

But the transformation you undergo in 2026 won't end when the calendar changes.

The person you become during this Fire Horse year, the clarity you gain, the courage you build, the alignment you create, that stays with you.

You'll carry it into 2027, 2028, and beyond.

The work you do now creates the foundation for everything that comes next.

REMEMBER WHO YOU ARE

Before you close this guide, I want to remind you of something important. You didn't find this book by accident.

You found it because something inside you knew you were ready.

Ready to stop waiting.

Ready to stop playing small.

Ready to step into the fullness of who you're meant to be.

The Fire Horse year is your invitation to claim that power.

Not someday. Now.

You are *not* too late.

You are *not* unprepared.

You are *not* unworthy.

You are exactly where you need to be.

And you are ready.

ADDITIONAL SUPPORT FOR YOUR JOURNEY

This guide gives you everything you need to prepare for the Fire Horse year on your own. But sometimes, personalized guidance can deepen your transformation.

If you'd like support from a professional Feng Shui consultant, someone who can look at your unique space, your specific challenges, and your personal energy, I'm here to help.

I offer personalized Coaching and Feng Shui consultations where we'll work together to optimize your life for the Fire Horse year and beyond.

Book a free exploration call with me to learn how Feng Shui can specifically help you. Send me an email to ana@ana-barreto.com

FREE FIRE HORSE MEDITATION

To support your journey, I've created a special Fire Horse Meditation designed to help you connect with the energy of 2026, release what no longer serves you, and anchor your intentions for the year ahead.

This guided meditation is a beautiful complement to the work you've done in this guide.

Access your free Fire Horse Meditation here: https://shorturl.at/aeaAy

Use it as often as you need, before February 17 to prepare, on the day itself to welcome the Fire Horse, or anytime during the year when you need to reconnect with your intentions and recenter your energy.

I create and release new meditations every month, often because a client, friend, or family member needs support. If you'd like to be alerted and receive these practices as they're released, I invite you to join my community and sign up for my newsletter. Visit www.ana-barreto.com.

A BLESSING FOR YOUR JOURNEY

As you step into the Fire Horse year, I offer you this blessing:

May you move through 2026 with courage and grace.

May you trust yourself even when the path is unclear.

May you release what no longer serves you and welcome what does.

May you recognize the doors that are meant for you and have the wisdom to walk through them.

May you find support when you need it, clarity when you seek it, and strength when you call for it.

May you remember that you are never alone, that the Fire Horse carries you, the Sheep protects you, and your own inner wisdom guides you.

And may you emerge from this year transformed—stronger, clearer, and more aligned with your truth than ever before.

Go Forward

The Fire Horse is waiting.

Not with judgment. Not with fear.

But with an invitation.

It's asking: Are you ready to rise?

And you already know the answer.

Yes.

You are ready.

Now go. Do the work. Trust the process.

And let the Fire Horse carry you forward into the most powerful year of your life.

With love and belief in your journey,

Ana Barreto

The End

ABOUT THE AUTHOR

Ana Barreto knows what it means to transform your life from the inside out.

A Brazilian American author, transformational teacher, coach, and certified Feng Shui consultant with more than 22 years of experience, Ana bridges the ancient wisdom of Eastern philosophy with the practical demands of modern life. Her approach is grounded, practical, and deeply spiritual. She blends her business expertise (a bachelor's degree in business, an MBA, and 36+ years in corporate leadership) with decades of inner work, mindfulness, and hands-on experience guiding the people who have sought her support, offering a transformational approach rooted in clarity, compassion, psychology, and wisdom.

As the founder of the Body, Mind & Wisdom Academy for Women, Ana guides women to break free from limiting patterns, restore inner peace, and step into the most empowered version of themselves. Although she works with men, she specializes in helping women shift the emotional, mental, and environmental patterns that keep them stuck. Ana works with their mindset, career goals, home support, relationships, and spirituality.

Her work goes far beyond surface-level fixes. Through personalized consultations, Ana helps clients align their physical spaces with their deepest intentions, creating homes that support healing, prosperity, and meaningful transformation. Her mindfulness teachings and spiritual practices are designed to fit gently into real life, helping busy women release self-sabotaging behaviors and cultivate clarity, confidence, and purpose.

Ana is the author of nine published books, each offering practical wisdom and soulful guidance to help women navigate life's challenges with strength and grace. Through her master classes, online courses, meditations, and motivational talks, she has empowered thousands of women around the world to create lives rooted in authenticity, joy, and intention.

When she's not teaching or writing, Ana enjoys cooking, traveling, hiking, biking, and kayaking, often alongside her partner, Jim, and spending time with her children, family, and friends.

Ready to work with Ana?

Explore her transformational programs, including Master Classes, Individual and Group Coaching, Feng Shui Consultations (in-person and virtual), Online Courses, Meditations, and Motivational Talks at www.ana-barreto.com/working-together.

www.ingramcontent.com/pod-product-compliance
Lightning Source LLC
LaVergne TN
LVHW051839080426
835512LV00018B/2968